# English Code 5

## Grammar Book

# Contents

# Welcome!

**1**  **Watch. Complete the sentence.**

anything   everyone   no one   nothing   someone

_____ wants to play the games with Sophia.

**2** **Read and write T (True) or F (False). Then circle the correct category for the underlined word or phrase in each sentence. Watch to check.**

**1** Sophia is <u>a robot</u> that can do many things. _____

    **a** somewhere     **b** something     **c** someone

**2** Sophia can explore <u>under the sea</u>. _____

    **a** something     **b** someone     **c** somewhere

**3** Sophia says, "Let's meet <u>the players</u>." _____

    **a** someone     **b** something     **c** somewhere

**4** Avatar is on vacation <u>in space</u>. _____

    **a** somewhere     **b** someone     **c** something

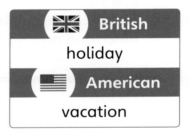

| 🇬🇧 British |
|---|
| holiday |
| 🇺🇸 American |
| vacation |

**3** **Look at the table. Write four coded sentences for your partner to guess and then check using the table.**

## CODE CRACKER

_B3-A1 in my class likes Avatar!_

_____

_____

_____

_____

|  | **A1** | **A2** | **A3** |
|---|---|---|---|
| **B1** | somewhere | no one | everywhere |
| **B2** | anyone | nothing | everything |
| **B3** | everyone | something | nowhere |
| **B4** | anything | anywhere | someone |

# Language lab

-WHERE, -ONE, -THING

## 1 Look at the picture and read the story. What was different about the vacation? Check ☑.

1   The family traveled to a strange country.  ☐

2   The family stayed in an unusual place.  ☐

3   The family met people with colorful names.  ☐

Last year my family went on a vacation to Spain. We didn't stay in a hotel. We stayed in an apartment in the center of Valencia! There are many apartment buildings in Valencia where anyone can stay.

We didn't know if the apartment was good or bad. Everyone was very surprised when we opened the door. It was so beautiful and the rooms had different colors, like red and blue.

Our apartment was on the first floor. A Spanish family lived next door to us. We spent a lot of time together. They showed us almost everything in Valencia and one night they cooked something for us. It was a traditional Spanish food called "paella"!

Everywhere we went in Valencia was great. I really liked the names of the streets. They sound so nice! For example, our street was Calle San Bruno. It was near a square called Plaza Don Bosco and near a park called Parque de Marxalenes. I loved it!

## 2 Read and circle T (True) or F (False).

1   The family wanted to stay in a hotel somewhere in the center of Valencia.  T / F

2   Anyone can stay in an apartment in Valencia.  T / F

3   No one in the family thought the apartment looked nice.  T / F

4   The family next door cooked something that people in Spain usually eat.  T / F

**Everyone** enjoys going to the beach.
We liked **everything** we saw.
We looked for it **everywhere**.

He was **someone** important.
They cooked **something** for us.
We stayed **somewhere** new.

**Anyone** can see that the sky is blue!
He was full and didn't want to eat **anything**.
We can go **anywhere** we like on vacation.

**No one** in my family enjoyed the food.
There was **nothing** to do.
There is **nowhere** to go.

**3** Read the text on page 4 again and underline words beginning with every-, some-, and any-.

**4** Read and match.

1 I was bored.
2 I'm hungry.
3 I can't do my homework.
4 We have a ball.
5 I dropped a glass of milk.
6 I'm a friendly person.

a It went everywhere on the floor.
b I need someone to help me.
c I had nothing to do.
d I can chat with anyone I meet.
e We need somewhere to play basketball.
f I need something to eat.

**5** Complete the rules with the missing words.

people   places   things

1 We use *everyone*, *someone*, *anyone*, and *no one* with _____ .
2 We use *everything*, *something*, *anything*, and *nothing* with _____ .
3 We use *everywhere*, *somewhere*, *anywhere*, and *nowhere* with _____ .

**6** Underline the mistakes and correct the sentences.

1 You can ask <u>everything</u> to help you.
   *You can ask someone to help you.*
   _____

2 I'm thirsty, can I have someone to drink?
   _____

3 This place is boring, there's everywhere to go!
   _____

4 Something likes Sonia. She's very friendly and funny.
   _____

5 You feel lonely when you have everyone to talk to.
   _____

6 Somewhere is knocking on the door. Can you open it?
   _____

7 He came here because he didn't have nowhere to stay.
   _____

# Time for school

**1** 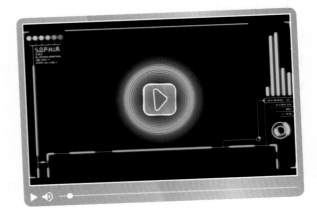 **Watch. What is Avatar's task for the math challenge? Check ☑ .**

1 Avatar must play some music. ☐

2 Avatar must not fall off. ☐

3 Avatar must answer a problem. ☐

**2** **Read and circle. Watch to check.**

1 Avatar (must) / must not walk on the two benches.

2 Avatar (must not) / must get the answer wrong.

3 I (must) / mustn't answer this problem.

4 You (must not) / must play some music on the piano.

| 🇬🇧 British | 🇺🇸 American |
|---|---|
| sum | problem |

**3** **Look at the rules. What happens if you don't follow them? Choose and write the correct result.**

## CODE CRACKER

Someone will be unhappy.   It will get lost.   People won't know we're students here.
Our books will get dirty.   We won't listen to what the teacher says.
The teacher will need to stop when we come in.

| Rules | Results |
|---|---|
| 1 We must wear the school uniform. | |
| 2 We mustn't eat or drink in the classroom. | |
| 3 We must keep our classroom equipment tidy. | |
| 4 We mustn't be late for class. | |
| 5 We mustn't use cell phones in class. | |
| 6 We must be kind to our classmates. | |

# Language lab 1

EXPRESSING RULES WITH *MUST*

I will express rules using **must** and **mustn't**.

**1** **Look at the pictures and read. Which sentence matches the story best? Check ☑ .**

1   The signs tell Lucy that people mustn't do anything in their town. ☐

2   The signs help Lucy know what people must or mustn't do. ☐

3   The signs show only what people must do in Winston. ☐

Hi, I'm Lucy and today I'm walking around my town, Winston! I'm looking for signs that tell us what to do or what not to do. It's for a school project.

I saw the No Running sign in a café. Children mustn't run around the tables.

The No Talking sign was on the wall in the quiet part of the library. It means you mustn't talk. Shh!

We saw the No Food and Drinks sign in the museum. You mustn't eat or drink there.

The Danger sign was outside a factory. It means you must be careful!

I saw the No Cell Phones sign in the movie theater. You mustn't use your phone when you watch a movie.

I saw the STOP sign on the street. Drivers must stop here before they drive on. If they don't, it's very dangerous.

There are so many rules.

**2** **Read again. Circle T (True) or F (False).**

1   You must run in the café.                     T / F

2   You must be quiet everywhere in the library.                              T / F

3   You must use your phone at the movie theater.                          T / F

4   You mustn't eat in the museum.        T / F

I **must** stay out of this building.
You **must** wear a helmet.

He **mustn't** go in there.
We **mustn't** run there.

**3** **Read again. Underline sentences with must and mustn't.**

## 4 Circle the correct word.

1 You (must) / mustn't wear a helmet at the skate park.

2 Students (must) / mustn't text during the lesson.

3 You (must) / mustn't be home before dinner time.

4 You (must) / mustn't talk when the principal is talking.

5 We (must) / mustn't run here! The floor is wet.

## 5 Read the sentences and answer the questions.

a You must be careful.

b You mustn't skateboard here.

1 Which sentence tells you not to do something? ____

2 Which sentence tells you to do something? ____

3 What form of the verb comes after *must*? verb with *to* / verb with *-ing* / verb without *to* or *-ing*

## 6 Order the words to make sentences.

1 library / You / mustn't / at the / talk / loudly

_____ .

2 skate park / wear / a helmet / at the / You / must

_____ .

3 go / into / You / that / area / mustn't

_____ .

4 mustn't / You / that / door / go / through

_____ .

## 7 Play a game in pairs.

A is a museum visitor and B is a guard at the museum. Look at the signs. A does one of the actions and B tells A what he/she must or mustn't do.

## 8 Design a sign and write the rule for it.

_____

# Language lab 2

EXPRESSING RULES WITH *HAVE TO*

> *I will talk about obligations using **have to** and **don't have to**.*

## 1 Read the dialogue. Circle T (True) or F (False).

**Lucas:** Hi! I'm Lucas. Are you new?

**Mary:** Hello! I'm Mary. Yes, this is my first day at this school.

**Lucas:** I'm sure you will like it here, but you have to follow the rules.

**Mary:** Can you tell me some of the rules?

**Lucas:** Sure, the most important rule is you have to be at school on time.

**Mary:** That won't be a problem for me.

**Lucas:** Secondly, you have to wear the correct school uniform every day.

**Mary:** That's good to know. Do I have to come to school on Saturdays?

**Lucas:** No, you don't. Only the swimming team has training on Saturdays.

**Mary:** How do I join the swimming team?

**Lucas:** You have to put your name on the list.

**Mary:** Thanks for the information, Lucas!

1 All students have to go to school on Saturday.  T / F

2 Lucas has to wear his school uniform every day.  T / F

3 Mary has to be at school on time.  T / F

4 Lucas doesn't have to follow the school rules.  T / F

## 2 Circle the correct words.

1 Miguel (have to clean) / has to clean his room.

2 I (don't have) / doesn't have to do my homework tonight.

3 Does Jessica (have) / have to go to bed early every day?

4 Students have to (wearing) / wear their uniforms at school.

---

You **have to** be at school on time.
Mary **has to** wear her uniform.

You **don't have to** take the school bus.
He **doesn't have to** go to bed early.

**Do** I **have to** stay after school?
Yes, you **do**. / No, you **don't**.

**Does** he **have to** do homework?
Yes, he **does**. / No, he **doesn't**.

---

## 3 Complete the sentences with the correct form of have to.

1 You _____ help your friend with homework if she doesn't understand something.

2 Eva and Mark _____ take the bus to school. They can walk.

3 _____ study hard when he has an exam?

# 2 Landscapes of China

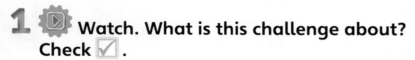

**1**  **Watch. What is this challenge about? Check ☑.**

questions about the past ☐

questions about the present ☐

questions about the future ☐

**2** **Read and circle. Watch to check.**

1 Which country ( did invent / invented ) fireworks?

2 When did the ancient Chinese ( invent / invented ) paper?

3 They ( invented / did invent ) paper around 100 BCE.

4 What did artists ( painted / paint ) in ancient China?

**3** **Read the answers. Write the correct question word.**

## CODE CRACKER

what (2)   when   where   which   who

1 They painted beautiful <u>landscapes</u>. _____

2 They invented paper <u>around 100 BCE</u>. _____

3 <u>China</u> invented fireworks. _____

4 I read a book <u>at the library</u>. _____

5 <u>Confucius</u> said that. _____

6 They ate <u>duck with rice</u>. _____

# Language lab 1

QUESTIONS ABOUT THE PAST

> I will ask questions about the past.

## 1 Read the dialog. Who did Max spend his vacation with?

his grandparents ☐    Lucia ☐    his friend Jack ☐

**Max:** Hi, Lucia! I didn't see you this summer. Where were you?

**Lucia:** My family went to China.

**Max:** That sounds great! What did you do?

**Lucia:** We visited many places and we walked along the Great Wall! Did you know that it's the longest building in the world? We even learned some Chinese words!

**Max:** Who taught you the words?

**Lucia:** Well, we had a guide with us, Li Wei. He told us so many things about China and its history. He was amazing. So, tell me about your vacation. What did you do?

**Max:** I went to a summer camp in Italy.

**Lucia:** Cool! When did you go?

**Max:** I went in July. I had a great time. I played soccer and volleyball. I went horseback riding in the mountains and canoeing on the river. I learned to play water polo, too!

**Lucia:** Who did you go with?

**Max:** I went with my friend Jack. Unfortunately, the summer camp was too short! The rest of the summer wasn't so much fun. My parents wanted me to review math for school, so I had to do some review work every day.

**Lucia:** Oh, no! Poor you!

## 2 Read again. Circle T (True) or F (False).

1 Max is Lucia's brother.                     T / F
2 Lucia visited the Great Wall of China.       T / F
3 Max didn't enjoy the summer camp.            T / F
4 Lucia spent the summer by the ocean.         T / F
5 Max thinks the summer camp was too short.    T / F

## 3 Read again. Underline wh- questions.

### Object questions

**Where did** you **spend** your vacation?

**When did** you **see** Ben?

**How did** you **learn** some Chinese words?

**Which country did** you **visit**?

### Subject questions

**Who traveled** with you to Spain?

**What happened** on your vacation?

## 4 Read and circle.

1   Where ( did Lucia stay ) / Lucia stayed on her vacation?

2   Who ( did go ) / went horseback riding with you?

3   When ( you woke up ) / did you wake up at the camp?

4   What ( happened ) / did happen on your trip to China?

5   Who ( did teach ) / taught you Chinese words?

## 5  Read and match the sentences to the rules.

1   What did you enjoy at summer camp?

2   Who saw the Great Wall of China?

a   To ask a question in the past when we know who performed the action, we use *did*.  _____

b   To ask a question in the past when we don't know who or what performed the action, we don't use *did*.  _____

## 6 Write five questions using the correct form of the words below.

1   who   visit you   last week

1 _____ ?

2   what   have for lunch with your family   this weekend

2 _____ ?

3   when   go to the beach with your friends   last time

3 _____ ?

4   where   spend your winter break   last year

4 _____ ?

5   how   get to (your) school   yesterday

5 _____ ?

## 7  Work with a partner. Take turns asking and answering the questions in 6.

Who visited you last week?

My cousin Jeremy visited me last week!

# Language lab 2

QUESTIONS ABOUT THE PAST

I will ask questions about what life was like in the past.

## 1 Read and write the questions with the words.

### THE GREAT WALL OF CHINA

The Great Wall is a very long wall in China. It's about 21,196 kilometers long. It's the longest thing people built in the world. It's also very old! It took more than 200 years to finish it.

**When did people build the Great Wall?**

People in China started building the wall over 2,000 years ago.

**What did people use to build the Great Wall?**

They used rocks and dirt at first. Then during the Ming Dynasty they used bricks. They built the wall to protect their country.

Along the wall there are thousands of watch towers. These were high buildings where soldiers used to stand. They sent smoke signals when there was danger.

1  _____ ? (which)

   The Great Wall is the longest building in the world.

2  _____ ? (what)

   People in China used materials like rocks to build the Great Wall.

3  _____ ? (which)

   The Ming Dynasty used bricks to complete the Wall.

4  _____ ? (what)

   Soldiers sent signals of smoke when there was danger.

## 2 Order and write questions.

1  wear   you   did   what   clothes   yesterday

   _____ ?

2  you   did   see   movie   week   last   which

   _____ ?

3  week   class   enjoy   you   did   last   which

   _____ ?

> **Which** materials **did** the Chinese **use** to build the Great Wall?
>
> **What** signals **did** Chinese soldiers **send**?

## 3 Work with a partner. Take turns asking and answering the questions in 2.

What clothes did you wear yesterday?   I wore my blue and red dress!

# 3 Hanging out

**1** ▷ **Watch. What is the player doing next month? Check ☑.**

1 She is riding a bike. ☐

2 She is going on vacation. ☐

3 She is going bowling. ☐

**2** ▷ **Complete with the correct form of be and the words from the box. Watch to check.**

1 I _____ in the park on Tuesday.

2 I _____ to a concert tomorrow evening.

3 In the morning I _____ a kite.

4 _____ you _____ next month?

> fly   go
> play tennis
> skateboard

**3** 💬 **Look. Code three sentences for your partner to say.**

## CODE CRACKER ⚙️⚙️⚙️

3 ■ 5 ● 2 ▲

I am playing basketball tomorrow.

Correct!

| | | ■ | ● | ▲ |
|---|---|---|---|---|
| **1** | we | take a test | next weekend |
| **2** | she | make popcorn | tomorrow |
| **3** | I | meet a friend | next month |
| **4** | they | go to the movies | this week |
| **5** | he | play basketball | this morning |

_____

_____

# Language lab 1

**FIXED FUTURE PLANS**

> *I will talk about fixed plans for the future.*

## 1 Look at the picture and read. Choose the best subject for the email. Write.

1 I can't wait for this vacation to end!

2 Having a great time in Florida!

3 Fun on the weekend

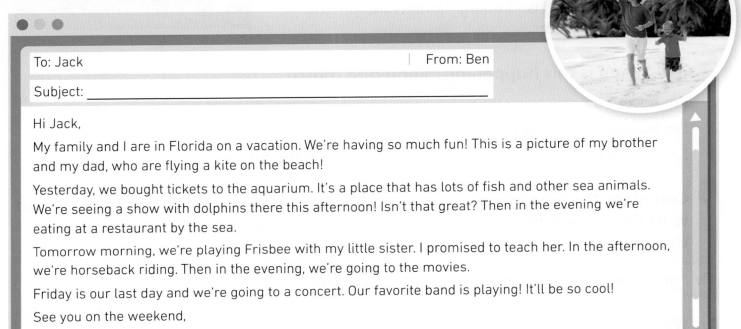

To: Jack             | From: Ben

Subject: _____

Hi Jack,

My family and I are in Florida on a vacation. We're having so much fun! This is a picture of my brother and my dad, who are flying a kite on the beach!

Yesterday, we bought tickets to the aquarium. It's a place that has lots of fish and other sea animals. We're seeing a show with dolphins there this afternoon! Isn't that great? Then in the evening we're eating at a restaurant by the sea.

Tomorrow morning, we're playing Frisbee with my little sister. I promised to teach her. In the afternoon, we're horseback riding. Then in the evening, we're going to the movies.

Friday is our last day and we're going to a concert. Our favorite band is playing! It'll be so cool!

See you on the weekend,

Ben

## 2 Read again. Answer the questions. Circle T (True) or F (False).

1 Ben is seeing a show at the aquarium today.    T / F

2 Ben is eating at a restaurant near the sea this evening.    T / F

3 Ben is going horseback riding tomorrow morning.    T / F

4 Ben is going to a concert on the weekend.    T / F

> **I'm playing baseball** tomorrow.
> She**'s bowling** next week.
>
> **I'm not horseback riding** to the concert tomorrow.
> He **isn't flying kites** next week.
>
> **Are** you **playing Frisbee** on the weekend?
> Yes, I **am**. / No, I**'m not**.

## 3 Read again. Underline verbs about the future ending in *-ing* in blue and about the present in green.

## 4 Circle the correct answer.

1 ( We're staying / We stay ) at a hotel this summer.

2 Tomorrow, ( I'm visiting / I visit ) my grandmother.

3 ( I'm leaving / I left ) next Monday.

4 ( He has / He's having ) a party next week.

5 ( They had / They're having ) a class meeting tomorrow morning.

6 We ( aren't doing / isn't doing ) homework tonight. We're playing soccer.

## 5 When is this happening? Read and match.

1 I'm having a party tomorrow.

2 I'm having a party right now.

3 I'm having a party.

a at the moment

b can be at the moment or in the future

c in the future

## 6 Complete the sentences with the correct form of the words.

fly   go   meet   not go   take   visit

1 We _____ a test tomorrow.

2 I _____ my uncle next week.

3 She _____ to the movies on Friday. She has other plans.

4 _____ your friend at the park tomorrow?

5 I _____ kites on the beach next week.

6 He _____ to a concert tomorrow afternoon.

## 7 What are you doing next week? Plan your activities. Then tell your partner.

do homework   fly a kite   go bowling
go to school   go to the movies   play baseball
play Frisbee   ride your scooter   roller-skate   swim

| | morning | afternoon | evening |
|---|---|---|---|
| **Monday** | go to school | | |
| **Tuesday** | | | |
| **Wednesday** | | | |
| **Thursday** | | | |
| **Friday** | | | |

What are you doing next week?

I'm going to school on Monday morning.

# Language lab 2

TIME PHRASES

I will talk about when things are happening.

## 1 Look at the brochure and write the times.

|  | Monday | Tuesday | Wednesday |
|---|---|---|---|
| dancing | 9:45 – 11:15 |  |  |
| Frisbee |  | 10:00 – 11:00 | 10:30 – 11:15 |
| kites |  | 12:00 – 2:00 |  |
| swimming |  |  | 12:30 – 2:15 |
| restaurant | 1:00 – 2:30 |  |  |

half past twelve    half past two    noon    quarter past eleven    quarter to ten    ten o'clock

Welcome to this year's Summer Festival! We have so many special things for you to do this year!

On Monday we're dancing at
1 _____ and then we're eating at a beach restaurant between one o'clock and 2 _____ . Tuesday will be a fantastic day, too! We're playing Frisbee on the beach between 3 _____

and eleven o'clock and then at
4 _____ we're flying kites!

The last day is Wednesday. Don't be sad, because we're playing Frisbee again between half past ten and 5 _____ .
Then we're swimming between
6 _____ and quarter past two! See you all at the beach!

## 2 Circle the correct word.

1   They're scooting  between / at  noon and half past one.

2   I'm playing Frisbee at quarter  three / past three  tomorrow.

3   Eva's bowling between eleven o'clock and  half past / half  twelve.

I'm swimming **at half past twelve.**

We're going to the movies **between noon and quarter to two.**

## 3 Order the words to write sentences.

1   skateboarding    at    at the park    past    She's    two    half

_____ .

2   quarter    He's    to    the movies    eight    going to    at

_____ .

3   Mary and Emily    noon    one    are flying    between    and    kites    o'clock

_____ .

# 4 Movie magic

**1** 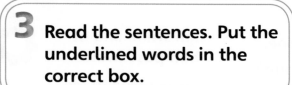 **Watch. What do the players find out in this challenge? Underline.**

1   the worst and the longest movie for Avatar

2   the saddest and the scariest movie for Avatar

3   the funniest and the best movie for Avatar

**2** 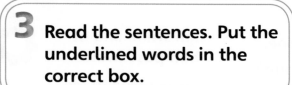 **Read and complete with the words. Watch to check.**

> funnier   good   the best   the funniest

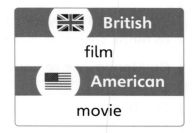

| 🇬🇧 | **British** |
|---|---|
| | film |
| 🇺🇸 | **American** |
| | movie |

1   Avatar thinks *Coco* is _____ movie.

2   Avatar thinks *Coco* is _____ than *Moana*.

3   *Frozen*, *Paddington*, and *Willy Wonka* are all _____ movies.

4   I think *Toy Story 4* is _____ movie.

**3** **Read the sentences. Put the underlined words in the correct box.**

## CODE CRACKER

| + | ++ | +++ |
|---|---|---|
| | | |

1   *Shrek* is the best movie of all. *The Jungle Book* is a good movie. *Toy Story 4* is better than *The Jungle Book*.

2   Mat is funnier than Jeremy. Jeremy is a funny boy. Jack is the funniest of all.

3   Daisy is the cleverest of all. Jane is cleverer than Sue. Sue is a clever student.

4   Apples are sweet. Honey is the sweetest of all. Chocolate is sweeter than apples.

# Language lab 1

*I will compare things.*

MAKING COMPARISONS

## 1 Read. Which is the best title for the text? Check ☑.

1   A scary movie about aliens and dinosaurs  ☐

2   A science fiction movie you must watch  ☐

3   A movie that will only make you scared  ☐

### A movie review by Emma Harris

I love science fiction movies. Last week, I saw a movie called *Dinosaur X*. I watched it with my sister. I don't think dinosaurs are as frightening as aliens, but this movie was great. The director wasn't as talented as my favorite one, but he was OK.

The sound effects were really good and the script was even better than the sound effects. The special effects, however, were the best. You could feel the dinosaurs walking on the ground.

The most frightening scene was the one where two dinosaurs were chasing an actor. My sister thinks it wasn't as frightening as the scene where dinosaurs were fighting each other. But there were some funny moments too, like when a dinosaur was eating a banana. The funniest one was when a dinosaur wanted to drive a car and crashed it into a tree!

So, for great special effects and some frightening and funny scenes, watch *Dinosaur X*!

## 2 Read again. Circle T (True) or F (False).

1   For Emma, aliens are more frightening than dinosaurs.               T / F

2   The director of *Dinosaur X* was more talented than Emma's favorite director.   T / F

3   The special effects weren't as good as the sound effects.            T / F

4   A dinosaur driving a car was the funniest moment of the movie.       T / F

| Adjective | Comparative | Superlative |
|---|---|---|
| John is a **talented** director. | Gary is **more talented** than John. | Paul is the **most talented** director of all. |
| Kelly is a **funny** actor. | Kate is **funnier** than Kelly. | Sue is the **funniest** of all. |
| The music was **good / bad**. | The script was **better / worse** than the music. | The acting was the **best / worst** of all. |

*Dinosaur X* is / isn't **as funny as** *Monsters 2*.

**3** Read the text on page 19 again. Underline the words and phrases that compare.

**4** Circle the correct word.

1   The movie I saw yesterday was the most exciting / more exciting movie of all.
2   The animation wasn't as good / as good as the script.
3   *Sea Creature* was expensive / more expensive than *Space Danger*.
4   Peter Alan is the famous / the most famous actor in the movie.
5   The scene with the spiders was worse than / bad the scene with the shark.
6   I think science fiction is more interesting / the most interesting than comedy.

**5** Read the sentences and answer the questions.

1   Aliens are more frightening than dinosaurs.
2   Aliens are the most frightening characters of all.
3   Dinosaurs are more exciting than aliens.
4   Dinosaurs are the most exciting characters of all.

a   Which sentences compare all characters?          _____
b   Which sentences compare two kinds of characters?          _____

**6** Think about your favorite movie. Write about it using these words. Tell your partner about the movie.

> as good as   more boring than   more interesting than
> not as frightening as   the best   the funniest   the worst

1   _____
2   _____
3   _____
4   _____
5   _____

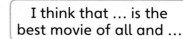

I think that … is the best movie of all and …

# Language lab 2

## WHAT MIGHT HAPPEN

> I will talk about what might happen.

## 1 Read the dialog. Circle T (True) or F (False).

**Adam:** I'm a director and I also write scripts for movies. Some people believe that computers will be making movies from now on. They will program robots to act in movies, generate digital characters and special effects, and write scripts.

**Bella:** Might robots be the only actors?

**Adam:** Robots might play some simple characters. But there will always be characters and scenes that only people can play. For example, scenes with strong emotions. So, people will always have to play in movies.

**Ken:** Will there be scenes where human actors might play together with computer generated characters?

**Adam:** Well, in the future, human actors might play next to computer generated characters. There are a couple of movies today where this is true.

**Beth:** Might computers write scripts that are funnier than the ones people write?

**Adam:** Yes, I think that'll happen soon! We might make computers that can write scripts and act, but there will always have to be directors to tell computers how to film the scenes they write!

| | | |
|---|---|---|
| 1 | Computers might make movies in the future. | T / F |
| 2 | People might not play in scenes with emotions. | T / F |
| 3 | Computers might write scripts in the future. | T / F |

## 2 Read and match.

1 Computers might     a become directors.

2 There might     b make movies from now on.

3 Computers might not     c be scenes with both human and computer characters.

> Computers **might write** scripts.
>
> We **might not** need human actors in all scenes.

## 3 Order the words to write sentences.

1 be   as good as   the script   not   The animation   might

_____ .

2 *Happy Mouse*   funnier   be   your favorite movie   might   than

_____ .

# 5 Once in a lifetime

## 1 ▶ Watch. Where has Avatar climbed a mountain? Check ✓ .

Japan ☐    Costa Rica ☐

Saudi Arabia ☐    Egypt ☐

## 2 ▶ Read and complete. Watch to check.

1  **A:** Have you ever _____ (fly) in a hot air balloon?

   **B:** Yes, I've _____ (fly) over the great pyramids of Egypt.

2  Have you ever _____ (climb) a mountain?

3  Yes, I've _____ (see) toucans and frogs.

## 3 Read and sort. Add one more sentence to each category. Remember to use . or ? for each sentence.

## CODE CRACKER

Has he seen frogs   He's been to Costa Rica   Have you eaten sushi

He hasn't ridden a horse   Has she climbed Mount Fuji

I haven't flown in a hot air balloon   I've seen toucans

She's visited Egypt   You haven't visited the Great Pyramids

| + | – | ? |
|---|---|---|
|   |   |   |

# Language lab 1

TALKING ABOUT LIFE EXPERIENCES

> *I will talk about experiences I've had in my life.*

## 1 Read this blog post. What is it about? Check ☑.

1 things to do on the beach ☐

2 experiences for children ☐

3 where to go on vacation ☐

4 what to do when you're bored ☐

### Things children could do before they're 12

We asked some boys and girls these questions.

| Have you ever ... | Yes | No |
|---|---|---|
| 1 been camping? | | |
| 2 hiked up a mountain? | | |
| 3 been snorkeling? | | |
| 4 visited a palace? | | |
| 5 climbed up a tower? | | |
| 6 looked for shells at the beach? | | |
| 7 run around in the rain? | | |
| 8 flown in a hot air balloon? | | |

**Here are some of the answers.**

**Peter, 11 ½:** No, I have never hiked up a mountain and I have never been camping. But I have visited a palace and I have run around in the rain.

**Alicia, 11:** My parents love camping, so I have been camping many times. Of course, I have looked for shells at the beach and I have been snorkeling. It was the most fun I have ever had!

**What about you? Have you ever done any of these things?**

## 2 Read again. Complete the sentences with one word.

1 Alicia has _____ snorkeling and it was a lot of fun.

2 Peter _____ hiked up a mountain before.

3 Alicia _____ been camping.

4 Peter has _____ a palace before.

5 Alicia has _____ for shells on the beach.

| 🇬🇧 British | 🇺🇸 American |
|---|---|
| snorkelling | snorkeling |

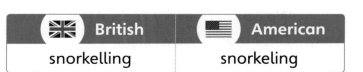

I **have traveled** by subway.
She **has seen** a bluebird.

You **haven't / have never traveled** by subway.
He **hasn't / has never seen** a bluebird.

**Have** you **ever ridden** a camel?
Yes, I **have.** / No, I **haven't.**

**Has** he **ever fed** a penguin?
Yes, he **has.** / No, he **hasn't.**

## 3 Read again. Underline the sentences with **ever** and **never**.

## 4 Circle the correct word.

1  A: So, your dad's a pilot! Have you (ever) / never flown in a plane?

   B: Yes, I have. But I have (never) / ever flown in a helicopter.

2  A: Have you (never) / ever climbed up a tower?

   B: Of course! Many times! But I have (ever) / never visited a palace.

**Watch out!**

go to (place) ➜ been to (place)

I've never been to France.

## 5 Read the dialog. Complete with the correct form of the words and ever or never when necessary.

**Meg:** Hi, Alan! My family and I are preparing for our summer vacation! We're going to Turkey. Have 1 _____ (you/go) to Turkey?

**Alan:** Hi, Meg. Wow, that's so cool! No, I 2 _____ (go) to Turkey. But I've been to Egypt and I've also ridden a camel. 3 _____ (you/ride) a camel?

**Meg:** No, I haven't. But I 4 _____ (ride) a horse.

**Alan:** Well, it's not quite the same! So, what will you do in Turkey?

**Meg:** Well, we're going to fly in a hot air balloon and I'm so excited! 5 _____ (you/fly) in a hot air balloon?

**Alan:** Yes, I have. There's a hot air balloon festival near the town where my cousin lives. We go there every year! After that we always hike up the mountain.

**Meg:** Oh, I didn't know. 6 _____ (go) camping? We're going camping in Turkey, but I'm afraid of all the insects.

**Alan:** Don't worry! I've been camping many times before. You'll love it.

**Meg:** I hope so!

## 6 Work with a partner. Has he/she ever done any of these things? Ask and answer.

climb up a tower   feed a horse
fly in a plane   go camping
go snorkeling   hike up a mountain
ride a camel   see an elephant
stay in a friend's house   travel by bus
visit a museum

Have you ever ridden a camel?

No, I haven't. I've never ridden a camel, but I've ridden a horse!

# Language lab 2

ASKING FOR INFORMATION

I will ask for information.

## 1 Read. Choose the best title for the blog post. Check ☑ .

My camping experience next to the Nile River ☐

My amazing vacation in Egypt ☐

Climbing up the Great Pyramid of Giza ☐

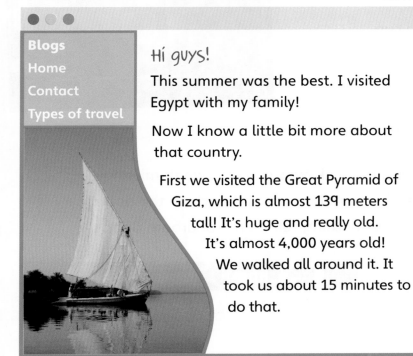

**Blogs**
**Home**
**Contact**
**Types of travel**

Hi guys!

This summer was the best. I visited Egypt with my family!

Now I know a little bit more about that country.

First we visited the Great Pyramid of Giza, which is almost 139 meters tall! It's huge and really old. It's almost 4,000 years old! We walked all around it. It took us about 15 minutes to do that.

I don't know if any of you have ever ridden a camel, but it was so much fun! Camels are lovely animals. It was a little expensive, $40 each, but it was worth it.

The best part of the trip was when we sailed along the Nile River. It's 6,650 kilometers long. It's one of the longest rivers in the world! The food was great and the people in Egypt are very friendly. If you haven't been, ask your parents to take you to Egypt next year!

Kathy

## 2 Read again and match.

1  How long is the Nile River?            a  almost 139 meters

2  How much does it cost to ride a camel?  b  6,650 kilometers

3  How tall is the Great Pyramid?          c  $40

## 3 Read the answers. Write the questions.

1  _____ ?

   The tower is 150 meters tall.

2  _____ ?

   The trip to Egypt takes one week.

3  _____ ?

   The palace is 100 years old.

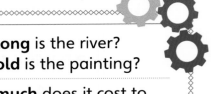

**How long** is the river?
**How old** is the painting?

**How much** does it cost to fly in a helicopter?
**How long** does the ride take?

# 6 Codes and clues

**1**  **Watch. What fell off Avatar's cupboard? Check ☑.**

a toothbrush ☐     a photo ☐     a cup ☐

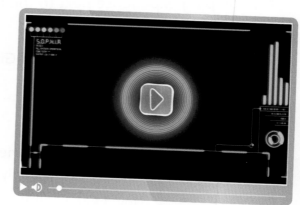

**2**  **Choose the correct words. Watch to check.**

1 Avatar was making cocoa ( when ) / after something strange happened.

2 Avatar was looking in the cookie jar when the milk ( was going ) / went missing.

3 Avatar ( was brushing ) / brushed his teeth when there was a knock on the door.

4 Avatar was doing exercise ( when ) / after something fell on the bedroom floor.

| 🇬🇧 **British** | 🇺🇸 **American** |
|---|---|
| biscuit tin | cookie jar |

**3** **Look at the sentences. Complete the boxes with the "long" events and the "short" events.**

## CODE CRACKER

1 Ben was snorkeling when he saw a big blue fish.

| A    snorkel | → | B    see a big blue fish |

2 I was riding a camel before I lost my earring.

| A | → | B |

3 When I dropped my camera, we were flying in a hot air balloon.

| A | → | B |

4 Sandra was hiking up a mountain when her sunglasses broke.

| A | → | B |

# Language lab 1

SHORT / LONG EVENTS IN THE PAST

> I will talk about two events happening in the past.

**1** **Read the article. How did Robert become a hero? Check** ☑ .

1   He found somebody's missing ring.   ☐

2   He helped his teacher get to the police station.   ☐

---

● ● ●

 **NEWS**          COMMENT   HOME   CONTACT

Ten-year-old Robert became a hero this morning. He and his class were visiting the railway museum after they had a lesson in history about steam trains last week.

The visit to the museum was great and it lasted an hour. Robert and his classmates were returning to the bus when Robert saw something shiny near a tree. "I was slowly walking toward the tree when the teacher told me to hurry up," says Robert. "At first I thought it was a piece of metal, but then I saw that it was a golden ring. I couldn't believe it!"

Robert gave the ring to his teacher and they took it to the police station. The police officer was talking on the phone when Robert and his teacher came in. When they showed the police officer the ring, he smiled happily. He asked, "What were you doing when you found it? An old lady was asking about a missing ring before you arrived!"

"We were leaving the museum when I saw it." said Robert.

"That's right! The old lady said she was walking around that area when she realized her ring was missing," said the police officer. He picked up the phone and called her. We're all proud of Robert.

---

**2** **Read again. Circle T (True) or F (False).**

1   Robert was returning to the bus when he saw something shiny.   T / F

2   Robert found a piece of metal in the grass.   T / F

3   Robert and his teacher went to the police station with the ring.   T / F

4   The old lady was at the police station when Robert went in.   T / F

> What **were you doing when / before / after** you found the earrings?
> I **was walking home when** I found the earrings.
> I **wasn't riding** my bike **when** I found the earrings.

**3** **Read again. Underline the sentences with** was/were + -ing.

27

## 4  Circle the correct word.

1   I ( was shopping ) / shopped  with my mom when I saw my friend.

2   A little boy  played  / ( was playing )  in the park when his mom called him.

3   Mary was leaving her home when she  ( was losing )  /  lost  her keys.

4   Who ( were you talking )  /  did you talk  to when I saw you yesterday?

5   He was playing volleyball when he  ( was breaking )  /  broke  his arm.

## 5  Andy is talking to his friend, Mark. Complete the dialog with answers (A–H). You don't need to use all the letters.

**Mark:**  Is your dad really a pilot?

**Andy:**  _D_

1   **Mark:**  Where did he fly yesterday?

**Andy:**  ____

2   **Mark:**  What time did he leave home?

**Andy:**  ____

3   **Mark:**  How did he get to the airport?

**Andy:**  ____

4   **Mark:**  What were you doing when he arrived in Paris?

**Andy:**  ____

5   **Mark:**  Are you going to be a pilot when you grow up?

**Andy:**  ____

A   At 7 in the morning. I was having breakfast when he left.

B   I was studying history at school. He arrived at 11 o'clock.

C   He was at home.

D   ~~Of course he is!~~

E   I don't know yet.

F   He doesn't like to fly to Paris.

G   He took the bus.

H   To Paris. He usually flies to Paris on Mondays.

## 6  Look at the table. Ask and answer with a partner. You can use when, after, and before.

| A | lose your book | find a wristwatch | see a bluebird | hear someone sing | break your glasses |
|---|---|---|---|---|---|
| B | hike up a mountain | do homework | fly in a helicopter | visit a palace | travel by subway |

What were you doing when you found a wristwatch?

I was hiking up a mountain when I found a wristwatch!

# Language lab 2

I will express how certain I am.

**HOW CERTAIN YOU ARE**

## 1 Read. Which bracelet are Ben and Lucy looking for? Check ☑.

**Ben:** Hey, Lucy. Mom called. She'll meet us outside the theater for the concert tonight. She wants her favorite bracelet … do you know which one it is?

**Lucy:** Hmm … Let's take a look in her bedroom.

**Ben:** Good idea. How about this green one? It must be her favorite. Look how shiny it is!

**Lucy:** It might be her favorite, but it can't be the one she wants. It's too expensive to wear to a concert!

**Ben:** You're right. This could be the one she wants. It's colorful and not too expensive.

**Lucy:** It can't be her favorite because I don't think she really likes it. Maybe it's this gold bracelet? What do you think, Ben?

**Ben:** Oh, no. She said "NOT the gold one," so it can't be the right one. What about this silver bracelet, that looks like a snake?

**Lucy:** Don't be silly! That's Dad's bracelet! It can't be this one.

**Ben:** Well, then it must be this one here. The silver one with the strange pattern.

**Lucy:** Yes, it must be the right one! Let's go, we're late!

| 🇬🇧 | British |
| --- | --- |
| | theatre |
| 🇺🇸 | American |
| | theater |

## 2 Read again and match.

1 To Lucy the green bracelet can't be the one

2 The colorful bracelet could be the one

3 It can't be the snake bracelet

a because it's not too expensive.

b because it's Dad's bracelet.

c because it's too expensive.

## 3 Circle the correct words.

1 You've been working all day. You (could / must) be tired.

2 There's a lot of sugar in that drink. It (can't / might) be good for your health.

3 He's not at school today. He (can't / could) be sick.

4 You (might / can't) be sleepy. You woke a minute ago.

You slept for 12 hours. You **can't be** tired.

The phone is ringing. It **might be** Helen.

Someone has my wristwatch. It **could be** Jeff.

You haven't eaten lunch. You **must be** hungry.

# 7 What shall we eat?

**1** 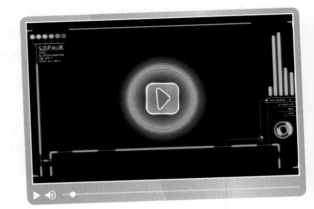 **Watch. What is the challenge about? Check ☑.**

sugar ☐     food ☐     a wire ☐

| 🇬🇧 British | 🇺🇸 American |
|---|---|
| fizzy drink | soda |

**2** **Complete with the correct form of the verbs. Watch to check.**

bake   make   mix   use

1  Sugar is _____ in many sodas.

2  Flour, eggs, and butter are _____ to make cakes.

3  Cake is _____ in an oven.

4  What is ice cream _____ of?

**3** **Look at the pictures. Which ingredient is missing? Circle. Then think of two more dishes. Create lists for your partner to complete.**

## CODE CRACKER

1  cake

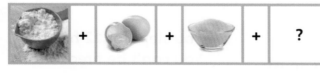

flour / sugar / butter / cream / eggs

2  ice cream

cream / flour / eggs / sugar / butter

3  _____

4  _____

# Language lab 1

PRESENT PASSIVE

I will learn to talk about actions without saying who does them.

## 1 Read the quiz. Circle the correct answers.

### What do you know about objects we use every day? Take this quiz and find out!

**1** Boxes like this are used to carry fruit. They are made of _____.

- **a** glass
- **b** plastic
- **c** wood
- **d** metal

**2** We get butter from cow's milk. It's used in a lot of _____.

- **a** vegetables
- **b** cakes
- **c** fruit
- **d** drinks

**3** Cans come in many colors. Usually _____ is drunk from them.

- **a** water
- **b** milk
- **c** tea
- **d** soda

**4** When we use bottles again, they are called "_____ material."

- **a** reopened
- **b** regrown
- **c** recycled
- **d** rebottled

**5** Tea is very popular all over the world. It was first grown in _____.

- **a** England
- **b** the USA
- **c** Iceland
- **d** China

**6** We wear socks in winter. They are made of _____.

- **a** rubber
- **b** wool
- **c** plastic
- **d** glass

## 2 Read and answer the questions with one or two words.

1 What is butter produced from? _____

2 Is milk drunk from a can? _____

3 What was first grown in China? _____

4 What is worn to keep our feet warm in winter? _____

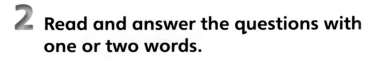

## 3 Read again. Underline the sentences where we don't say who does the action.

The box **is made** of wood.
Boots **are worn** when the weather is bad.

The box **isn't made** of metal.
Boots **aren't worn** when the weather is good.

**Is** water **drunk** from a bottle?
Yes, it **is**. / No, it **isn't**.
**Are** cans **used** for soda drinks?
Yes, they **are**. / No, they **aren't**.

## 4 Circle the correct word.

1  **A:**  What a nice vase! Who (made / make) it?

   **B:**  I'm glad you like it! My mom (makes / made) it.

   **A:**  What is it (make / made) of?

   **B:**  It's (made / make) of clay.

2  **A:**  What an interesting object! It looks old. Is it still (using / used)?

   **B:**  Yes, sometimes. It (comes / came) from Asia.

   **A:**  What (is / be) it used for?

   **B:**  It is (use / used) for playing music.

## 5  Read the sentences. Underline the correct words.

1  Daniel makes silver earrings. He's very good at it.

2  These earrings are made of silver. They're very expensive.

The meaning of the sentences is (similar / different).

The person who made the earrings is mentioned in sentence (1 / 2) because it's (not important / important).

## 6 Complete the sentences with the correct form of the words.

> make   mix   use   wear

1  The bucket _____ to clean houses.

2  The gloves _____ of rubber.

3  Flour _____ with eggs, butter,
   milk and sugar to make a cake.

4  T-shirts _____ by boys and girls
   all over the world.

## 7 Look up some recipes for your favorite food. Create your own simple recipe. Write it down without saying who does the actions. Share with a partner.

Apple Crumble: 10 Bramley apples <u>are peeled, cored and sliced</u>. Then, 2 table spoons of sugar <u>are added</u> and <u>mixed</u> with ...

# Language lab 2

TOO MUCH / MANY, ENOUGH / NOT ENOUGH

I will talk about quantities and order food.

## 1 Read. What food does Alexa enjoy most? Check ☑.

meat ☐  pasta and potatoes ☐  fish and rice ☐  cookies ☐

I'm Alexa. My brother, Tom, and I love running. We need to eat enough food to stay healthy because we run for a long time.

Tom eats a lot of meat, like chicken. But he also likes to eat pasta or potatoes with every meal. He says he doesn't eat enough chocolate or enough pancakes!

My favorite meal is fish and rice. Tom says I drink too much water, but I think he doesn't drink enough. I love eating fruit and vegetables. I also make sure I don't eat too many cookies.

Some people eat too much unhealthy food. They eat too many burgers and have soda with too much sugar in it. We like those things too, but only sometimes!

## 2 Read and circle T (True) or F (False).

| | | |
|---|---|---|
| 1 | Alexa enjoys eating vegetables. | T / F |
| 2 | Alexa likes fish and rice. | T / F |
| 3 | Alexa and Tom eat burgers every day. | T / F |
| 4 | Tom eats a lot of pancakes. | T / F |
| 5 | Tom thinks he doesn't eat enough chocolate. | T / F |

Tom says I drink **too much** water.
Some people eat **too many** burgers.

He doesn't eat **enough** fruit.
I eat **enough** vegetables.

## 3 Read the text again and underline sentences with too much, too many, and enough.

## 4 Circle the correct words.

1 We drink (too much) / too many / (enough) soda.

2 I think you eat (too much) / too many / (enough) sugar and it's not good for you.

3 I don't drink (too much) / too many / (enough) water when I run.

4 Some people eat (too much) / too many / (enough) candies.

5 Runners need to eat (too much) / too many / (enough) vegetables.

6 It's unhealthy to eat (too much) / too many / (enough) burgers.

# 8 Our digital world

**1** ▶ **Watch. How many sentences do they get correct? Check ☑ .**

one ☐  two ☐  three ☐

**2** ▶ **Read and complete with the correct tag questions. Watch to check.**

1 This app is boring, _____ ?

2 You like playing computer games about soccer, _____ ?

3 This TV show is really sad, _____ ?

| 🇬🇧 British | 🇺🇸 American |
|---|---|
| football | soccer |

**3** **Read and complete. Then use four questions to complete the dialog.**

can't   doesn't   it   they   you

1 Eric designs apps for cooking, _____ he?

2 You don't turn your devices off at night, do _____ ?

3 Liz can type on a keyboard fast, _____ she?

4 They always save their files, don't _____ ?

5 This is a microphone, isn't _____ ?

## CODE CRACKER ⚙️⚙️

A: Let's record a song for our project. We need a microphone and your guitar.

B: _____

A: Yes, it is. So, what do Eric and Liz do that they can use for their project? Do you know?

B: _____

A: Yes, he does. So, maybe they'll have a cooking project.

B: Maybe. I'm sure Liz will type the recipe.

A: _____

B: Yes, she can!

A: OK, let's save our file when we finish the song. I'm sure Eric and Liz do this, too.

B: _____

A: Yes, they always do.

# Language lab 1

TAG QUESTIONS

I will check information using tag questions.

## 1 Read the text. What does Ana want Michael to do? Check ☑.

**1** help her fix her camera ☐

**2** be in a video for her project ☐

**Ana:** Michael, I need your help with my school project.

**Michael:** Sure, Ana. What is your project about?

**Ana:** Well, I need to show a device I use a lot and what I use it for. That sounds easy, doesn't it? So I chose to present my camera and then show a video I made. It's a good idea, isn't it?

**Michael:** It is, Ana! So, what's the problem?

**Ana:** I don't know what kind of video to make. You can play a song on the guitar, can't you?

**Michael:** I can, yes … You don't want to make a video of me singing, do you?

**Ana:** I do! My camera has a very good microphone and I can record you many times. You want to choose the best video, don't you?

**Michael:** Of course, I do. OK, then. Let's try it. Press the button!

.....

**Ana:** OK, I've saved three files! Which is the best one?

**Michael:** Wait, let's connect my speaker to your camera. It sounds better, doesn't it?

**Ana:** Wow, it does! That's so cool!

**Michael:** I think the second video is the best. You like it, don't you?

**Ana:** Yes, I do! I'll download it onto my laptop and show it to the class tomorrow. Thanks, Michael!

**Michael:** Happy to help, Ana!

## 2 Read again. Circle T (True) or F (False).

1 Michael doesn't want to help Ana.          T / F
2 Ana's project is about computers.          T / F
3 Ana doesn't use her camera very often.     T / F
4 Ana likes to play the guitar and sing.     T / F
5 Michael chooses the second video.          T / F
6 Ana will show the video on her laptop.     T / F

This laptop **downloads** apps, **doesn't** it?
You **can record** songs, **can't** you?
They **are** old devices, **aren't** they?

This laptop **doesn't download** apps, **does** it?
You **can't record** songs, **can** you?
They **aren't** old devices, **are** they?

## 3 Read again. Underline sentences with tag questions.

## 4 Circle the correct word.

1. **A:** Hi Dad! My screen is not working! You can help me fix it, (can't you) / can you ?

   **B:** I can try. Let's see. You press this button to turn it on, don't I / (don't you) ?

   **A:** No, it's this one here.

   **B:** Sorry, it's a new laptop, (doesn't it) / isn't it ? OK, let's turn it off, then on.

   **A:** Hey, Dad! It's working! Thanks!

2. **A:** Downloading an app isn't very difficult, (isn't it) / is it ?

   **B:** You need a device, (don't you) / aren't you ?

   **A:** Yes. And a good internet connection can help, can it / (can't it) ?

   **B:** That's right! And you also need an app to download!

## 5 Complete the sentences with the correct tag questions.

1. Emily likes recording songs on her phone, _____ ?

2. You don't want me to turn off this device, _____ ?

3. He can type this text on the keyboard, _____ ?

4. These are the latest apps for listening to music, _____ ?

5. He doesn't have a wireless speaker at home, _____ ?

6. This isn't the screen that turns off by itself, _____ ?

## 6 💬 Work in pairs. How well do you know your partner? Ask and answer questions.

his/her age

have a microphone

know how to download an app

like pasta

like red

play an instrument

play computer games

sing well

You sing well, don't you?

Yes, I do. My turn. You don't like red, do you?

# Language lab 2

*-ING OR -ED?*

> I will describe things and say how things make me feel.

## 1 Read. How does lowercase music help Mark? Check ☑ .

1 He feels excited and it gives him energy for studying. ☐

2 It makes him feel relaxed and he can concentrate better. ☐

### LOWERCASE MUSIC by Mark

| Music | Comment | Home | Contact |

Hi guys! I've recently discovered lowercase music and I think it's amazing! It makes me feel relaxed and I listen to it when I do my homework. And do you know why? Because it's not exciting and it helps me concentrate. It means I can think about my homework and not anything else.

Lowercase is about sounds that we have around us. A musician called Steven Roden used paper to make different sounds, and then he used these sounds to make music. I was amazed when I read about this.

Some people say they feel frightened when they listen to lowercase, because they're not used to the sound of glass or paper. But I don't think it's frightening at all. Others say it's quite boring. But I disagree. The point of lowercase music is not to really listen to it, but to just let it play while you're doing other things ... like homework!

Why don't you try it?

## 2 Read again. Complete the sentences.

> amazing   exciting   frightening   relaxed

1 Mark thinks lowercase music is _____ .

2 When he listens to it he feels _____ .

3 Lowercase isn't _____ and Mark can concentrate.

4 Some people find the sounds of glass or paper _____ .

> This painting looks **frightening**.
>
> This music sounds **exciting**.
>
> I felt **frightened** when I saw the movie.
>
> This music makes me feel **excited**.

## 3 Complete the sentences.

1 Downloading an app can be long and _____ sometimes.

   When I am _____ I listen to my favorite music.

> bored   boring

2 This new video game looks _____ .

   I'm _____ that there are so many music apps.

> amazed   amazing

3 Are you _____ in technology and computers?

   The lesson about how computers started was very _____ .

> interested   interesting

# Extra Grammar 1

**SIMPLE PRESENT FOR SCHEDULED FUTURE EVENTS**

> *I will talk about scheduled future events using Simple Present.*

## 1 Read the text. Why has Mrs. Carter changed the class schedule? Circle.

1 because Tommy is late

2 because a teacher is not well

**Tommy:** Come on, Lizzy! We'll be late again!

**Lizzy:** I'm sorry! I can't walk any faster.

*Later …*

**Mrs. Carter:** Good morning, Tommy! Class starts at 8:15!

**Tommy:** Sorry, Mrs. Carter. My little sister walks too slowly.

**Mrs. Carter:** You should leave home earlier, then. Class, please remember that Ms. Perez, your Spanish teacher, is sick. So we have changed our schedule for this week.

**George:** When do we have music, Mrs. Carter?

**Mrs. Carter:** Tomorrow, from 9:55, instead of Spanish.

**May:** When do we have P.E.?

**Mrs. Carter:** On Thursday, as usual. P.E. doesn't change.

**Peter:** What about our school trip to the museum on Friday?

**Mrs. Carter:** Our school trip doesn't change. The school bus leaves at 7:30. Please make sure you're here on time because we can't wait.

## 2 Complete the sentences. Read again and check.

1 Classes _____ at quarter past eight every day.

2 Students _____ a music lesson tomorrow at 9:55.

3 P.E. _____ on Thursday and it won't change.

4 Students _____ for their trip to the museum at 7:30.

> have
> is
> leave
> start

## 3 Read the dialog again. Underline sentences in Simple Present which talk about future events.

> The music class **starts** at 9:55.
>
> They **go** to the museum on Friday.
>
> When **do** you **have** music this week?

38

## 4 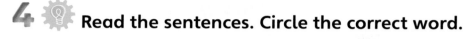 Read the sentences. Circle the correct word.

1  Hurry up! The movie starts in five minutes!

We use Simple Present to talk about events which (will happen) / happened .

Those events (are) / aren't based on calendars or timetables.

2  The mall opens at 7 o'clock.

## 5 Complete the text with the correct form of the words.

### New Classes at Sunny Summer Camp!

Sunny Summer Camp is pleased to announce that this year we're offering a soccer academy and new dance classes.

**Do you want your child to learn to play soccer?**

Classes at the Soccer Academy for 6 to 12 year olds 1 _____ (start) on Monday evening. Classes 2 _____ (last) from 5 p.m. to 7 p.m. Players aged 12 and over can play in a special league, which 3 _____ (begin) next Friday evening at 8:15. Practice 4 _____ (end) at 9:45.

**Are you interested in our dance classes?**

The Dance Academy 5 _____ (start) on Saturday morning for children aged 3–12. Classes 6 _____ (begin) at 9 a.m.

## 6 Make your own timetable for next week on a piece of paper. Look at your schedule and work with a partner. Ask and answer questions.

| Monday | Tuesday | Wednesday | Thursday | Friday | Saturday |
|--------|---------|-----------|----------|--------|----------|
|        |         |           |          | bike trip with class; we leave at 10 a.m. |          |

What do you have on Friday?

I have a bike trip on Friday. We leave at 10 in the morning!

# Extra Grammar 2

IF ... SENTENCES

I will learn to use different sentences with **if**.

## 1 Read. What body parts can you find? Underline.

○ ○ ○ ○ ○ ○ ○ ○ ○ ○ ○

Our bodies need oxygen to give power to our muscles. We do this by breathing, and it's quite simple.

If you don't breathe, you can't move! When you breathe, air goes in through your mouth and nose. The muscles in the top part of your body pull the air into your lungs. Here, the oxygen passes from the air into your blood. This is what moves around our bodies. The blood brings the oxygen to all your muscles, for example your stomach, your arms, your legs, and your brain.

If you exercise, you need more oxygen for your muscles, so you breathe more and your heart beats faster. You'll have strong lungs and a strong heart if you do enough exercise. You'll be able to get oxygen to your muscles fast. But if you don't work out, then you'll get tired and you'll get out of breath easily!

## 2 Read again and match.

1 When you breathe,
2 In your lungs, oxygen
3 If you don't do enough exercise,
4 Blood brings oxygen

a passes into your blood.
b you'll get out of breath easily.
c to your muscles.
d air goes into your lungs.

## 3 Read again. Underline sentences in Zero Conditional and circle sentences in the First Conditional.

**Zero Conditional**

Your heart **beats** faster if you **exercise**.

If you **don't breathe**, you **can't move**.

**First Conditional**

You**'ll have** strong lungs if you **exercise**.

If you **don't do** much exercise, you**'ll get** breathless easily.

## 4 Circle the correct word.

1 If she studies hard, she (will pass) / passes the test.

2 My brother doesn't like peanuts. If he eats them, he (will get) / gets sick.

3 If you (won't wear) / don't wear your coat, you'll be cold.

4 When the weather (is) / will be hot, I wear sandals.

## 5 Read the sentences and answer the questions. Then complete the rules with *Zero* or *First*.

1 If you exercise regularly, you get fit.

2 If you exercise too much, you'll feel tired.

a Which sentence is Zero Conditional? ____

b Which sentence is First Conditional? ____

c Which sentence is always true? ____

d Which sentence is about a real or possible situation? ____

In _____ Conditional we use *If* + Simple Present, and Simple Present.

In _____ Conditional we use *If* + Simple Present, and *will*.

## 6 Complete the sentences with the correct form of the words.

1 If dogs _____ (eat) chocolate, they _____ (get) sick.

2 If you _____ (mix) yellow and green, you _____ (get) blue.

3 If she _____ (not train), she _____ (not be) on the team.

4 If they _____ (walk) fast, they _____ (catch) the bus.

## 7 Play a game in pairs. A says the first part of the sentence and B the other part.

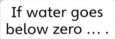
If water goes below zero … .

… it freezes!

| water goes below zero | freeze |
| drink very cold milk | teeth hurt |
| see my friend tomorrow | stop for a chat |
| weather is good | have a picnic |

# Extra Grammar 3

SUCH A / AN ... / SO ... THAT

> I will learn to use **such** and **so** with nouns and adjectives.

## 1 Read the dialog. What are the boys looking for? Check ✓.

shirts ☐    shoes ☐    jeans ☐

**Mom:** This shopping mall is such a busy place that you might get lost.

**Adam:** Oh, Mom! John and I are 15! We can go to the men's section and you can go shopping with the girls. We can meet here at 12 o'clock.

**Mom:** That's a good idea! Do you know where you want to go, Laura?

**Laura:** I'd like to look for a new dress. My dresses look so old that I don't want to wear them anymore.

**Mom:** OK, then! Marta and I need some jeans, don't we?

**Marta:** Yes, Mom. Laura, look at those dresses! They're so cool that I want them all!

**Laura:** Oh, that one over there is such a great color that I think I'll buy it for myself!

**Mom:** You're right, but look at the prices! This is such an expensive store that we might need to look somewhere else.

**John:** I need new sneakers. My shoes are so old that my feet hurt when I walk for a long time.

**Adam:** There are plenty of shoe stores on this level. Look! That store has a sale! What about those sneakers?

**John:** They're such nice sneakers that I definitely need to try them on! Let's go in!

## 2 Read again. Circle T (True) or F (False).

1 Laura's dresses are so new that she doesn't need to buy a new one.    T / F

2 The dress Laura likes is so expensive that she can't buy it.    T / F

3 John's shoes are so old that he can't walk well in them.    T / F

4 John doesn't want to try the sneakers on.    T / F

---

This dress is **so expensive that** I can't buy it.

The shopping mall is **such a busy place that** you can get lost.

They're **such nice sneakers that** I need to try them on.

**3** Read the dialog on page 42 again. Underline sentences with such an … that and so … that.

**4** Circle the correct word.

1  The movie I saw yesterday was (so good) / such good that I'll watch it again.

2  He's (such a bad) / so bad driver that he doesn't want to buy a car.

3  The food at this restaurant is such horrible / (so horrible) that nobody comes here to eat!

4  You're wearing so lovely / (such a lovely) dress that I want to buy the same one.

5  The book was so interesting / (such an interesting) that Paul read it in one day.

6  My feet are such big / (so big) that I can never find nice shoes.

7  She's so amazing / (such an amazing) person that everyone wants to be her friend.

**5** 🔅 Read the sentences. Circle the correct word.

A  The green sneakers are so comfortable that I can walk for hours in them.

B  This is such a pretty dress that I'll buy it right away.

*Such a/an* is followed by (a noun) / an adjective .

*So* is followed by a noun / (an adjective) .

**6** Complete the sentences with such a/an or so.

1  My friends are _____ interesting that I can talk to them for hours.

2  Tom has done _____ silly thing. He's going to get into trouble!

3  Have you ever eaten _____ awful salad?

4  The book my brother told me about is _____ good that I'll buy it.

5  My mom's _____ good cook that my friends love to come to dinner.

6  The present you chose for me is _____ expensive that I can't accept it.

# Grammar Reference

## Unit 1

### Language lab 1

*Must/Mustn't* for obligation:

I *must* do my homework.
I *mustn't* eat in the classroom.

You *must* practice at home.
You *mustn't* be late.

She *must* listen to the teacher.
He *mustn't* climb the wall.

They *must* take tests in school.
They *mustn't* forget the words.

### Language lab 2

*Have to* for obligation (affirmative and negative statements and questions):

You *have to* wear funny clothes and masks.
You *don't have to* act in the play if you're shy.

We all *have to* clean up after the play.
We *don't have to* juggle.

The drama teacher *has to* make posters.
She *doesn't have to* play music.

Do you *have to* learn to juggle?
No, you don't.

Do you *have to* wash the clothes after the play?
Yes, you do.

## Unit 2

### Language lab 1

Simple Past with *wh-* questions and irregular verbs in the Simple Past:

**Object Questions:**

*Where did* you go last Saturday?
I *went* to a castle.

*Who did* you meet there?
We *met* my aunt there.

*How did* you get there?
We *took* the bus.

*When did* you leave?
We *left* at five o'clock.

*What did* you do?
We *saw* the castle.

**Subject Questions:**

*Who went* with you?
I *went* with my family.

*What happened* next?
We *had* a picnic.

### Language lab 2

Simple Past questions with *what/which* + noun:

*What* food *did* you eat?
We ate cake in the café.

*Which* activity *did* you like best?
I liked playing sports from ancient times. It was fun.

# Unit 3

## Language lab 1

**Present Progressive for future plans (affirmative and negative statements and question form):**

Tomorrow, *we're going* on vacation.
*I'm not going* to the campsite in the afternoon.
*You're swimming* in the pool in the morning.
*He's walking* in the forest after lunch.
*They're playing* volleyball on Tuesday.

*Are you going* to the beach on Monday?
No, I'm not.

*Is Mom relaxing* tomorrow?
Yes, she is.

*Are the children eating* ice cream this evening?
Yes, they are.

## Language lab 2

**Phrases to talk about the time:**

I'm eating lunch *at noon*.
She's visiting the waterfall *between one o'clock and half past two*.
He's going horseback riding *at half past three*.
You're bowling *at quarter past five*.
We're playing in a concert *at quarter to eight*.
They're going to bed *at midnight*.

# Unit 4

## Language lab 1

**Comparative and superlative adjectives:**

*Panda Party* is *funnier than Ancient Times*.
*Paint With Me* is *more colorful than The Old House*.
*The Old House* is *as frightening as Tiger Trouble*.
*Ancient Times* isn't *as exciting as My Desert Vacation*.
*My Desert Vacation* is *the most interesting* book.
*Panda Party* is *the best* book ever!

## Language lab 2

***Might* for future possibilities:**

I *might* read *Tiger Trouble* next weekend.
My brother *might not* enjoy *The Old House*.
She *might* go to the bookstore after school.
We *might not* find an interesting book in the library.

# Grammar Reference

## Unit 5

### Language lab 1

**Present Perfect to talk about experiences (affirmative and negative sentences and question form):**

I *have been* to a theme park. I *haven't eaten* cotton candy. I *have never been* on a Ferris wheel.

He *has been* to the beach. He *hasn't walked* along the coast. He *has never explored* a cave.

*Have they ever ridden* a camel? No, they haven't.

*Has she ever stayed* in a hotel? Yes, she has.

*Has she ever hiked* up a mountain? No, she hasn't.

### Language lab 2

**Interrogatives with *how*:**

*How high is* the Ferris wheel? It's 80 meters high.

*How long does* it take to get to the theme park? It takes half an hour.

*How much does* it cost to visit the theme park? It costs $25.

## Unit 6

### Language lab 1

**Wh- questions using the Simple Past and Past Progressive:**

*What were you doing* when you *found* the secret waterfall? I *was exploring* the jungle when I *found* the secret waterfall.

*What were they doing* when they *saw* the turtles? They *were snorkeling* when they *saw* the turtles.

### Language lab 2

**Certainty and uncertainty:**

It *must be* a hummingbird because it is small and colorful. *I'm certain*.

It *might be* a secret waterfall because nobody lives near it. *I'm not sure*.

It *could be* his hat because he was wearing a hat earlier. *I think so*.
It *can't be* Saturday because we're at school. *I'm sure*.

# Unit 7

## Language lab 1

**Present Passive (affirmative sentences and question form):**

Soccer *is played* in lots of countries around the world.
Soccer fields **are found** in many towns and cities.

What are soccer balls made from?
Soccer balls **are made** from a type of plastic.

Is food sold at soccer games?
Yes, food *is sold* at soccer games.

Are soccer players paid a lot of money?
Yes, some soccer players **are paid** millions of dollars!

## Language lab 2

**Countable and uncountable nouns with *too much/too many/ enough/not enough*:**

I have *too much* popcorn.
He has *too many* hot dogs.
They have *enough* balls.
He doesn't have *enough* shoes!
She doesn't have *enough* water.

# Unit 8

## Language lab 1

**Tag questions (positive and negative):**

You like dancing, ***don't you***?
This dance class is fun, ***isn't it***?
Our teacher is great, ***isn't she***?
I'm not late, ***am I***?
We can enter the competition, ***can't we***?
Their clothes aren't uncomfortable, ***are they***?
He doesn't have a backache, ***does he***?

## Language lab 2

**Adjectives with *-ing* and *-ed* endings (describing objects and feelings):**

A competition? That sounds *exciting*. I feel *excited*.
The music is **relaxing**.
It makes me feel *relaxed*.
Their clothes look **interesting**. I'm *interested*.
That looks **tiring**. I feel *tired*!

**Pearson Education Limited**
KAO TWO
KAO Park
Hockham Way
Harlow, Essex
CMI7 9SR
England

and Associated Companies throughout the world.

english.com/englishcode

First published 2021
Second impression 2023
ISBN: 978-1-292-35455-2

Set in Heinemann Roman 12pt
Printed in Slovakia by Neografia

**Image Credits:**

**123RF.com:** Anatoly Fedotov 31, Anton Starikov 30, arcady31 7, 8, arcady32
8, Cathy Yeulet 36, cobalt 24, Gavril Bernad 5, Jacek Chabraszewski 33,
Jaren Wicklund 11, Kostic Dusan 16; **Pearson Education Ltd:** Jon Barlow
9, 12, 16, 20, 24, 28, 35, 36, 41, MindStudio 4; **Pearson India Education
Services Pvt. Ltd:** Sanjay Charadva 40; **Shutterstock:** 1968137 8, Africa
Studio 31, 32, Alexandr Makarov 31, all_about_people 37, Ambient Ideas
30, Andresr 39, Arcady 7, 7, aspen rock 41, bluebright 7, 8, Bombaert
Patrick 29, Creation 7, CREATISTA 32, 39, Ferenc Szelepcsenyi 42, Ivonne
Wierink 32, Jarno Gonzalez Zarraonandia 11, John Kasawa 29, kckate16
21, Khakimullin Aleksandr 19, LuckyPhoto 42, margouillat photo 31, Mike
Flippo 32, monticello 31, NadyaEugene 15, Ociacia 21, Oleksandr Lysenko
30, Ondrej Prosicky 22, Ortodox 31, Passakorn Umpornmaha 7, S_Photo 32,
Shutterstock 38, 39, siamionau pavel 43, Skylines 27, WH CHOW 25, Yuri
Yavnik 13

**Video Screenshots:** Jungle Creative

All other images © Pearson Education

**Cover Image:** *Front:* **Pearson Education Ltd:** Jon Barlow

MIX
Paper from
responsible sources
FSC™ C128612